CALL THE LIGHT

by Megan Pasnik

iiPUBLISHING

CALL THE LIGHT

Cover design by tonii

Illustrations: Original Artwork by Megan Pasnik

ISBN: 979-8-9850204-6-5

iiPUBLISHING
New York, NY
www.toniiinc.com

For my fellow humans across this earth who are choosing to embody their divinity in this lifetime.

For the medicine women, priestesses, shamans, healers, and witches who were never able to have their voices fully heard.

For the holy humans who stood for love and never lost faith.

For those who were persecuted for their pure intentions, those whose legacies have been burned and buried.

For my ancestors who never had the opportunities, freedom, and safety I have today but have because of them.

For the girls and the women of today who have been systematically forced to be silent, submissive, and aversive to their own sovereignty and empowerment.

For my guides who show me the way.

For my mother and father for showing me the fiercest and softest love I've ever known, and will never forget...

I AM HERE TO TALK ABOUT LOVE.

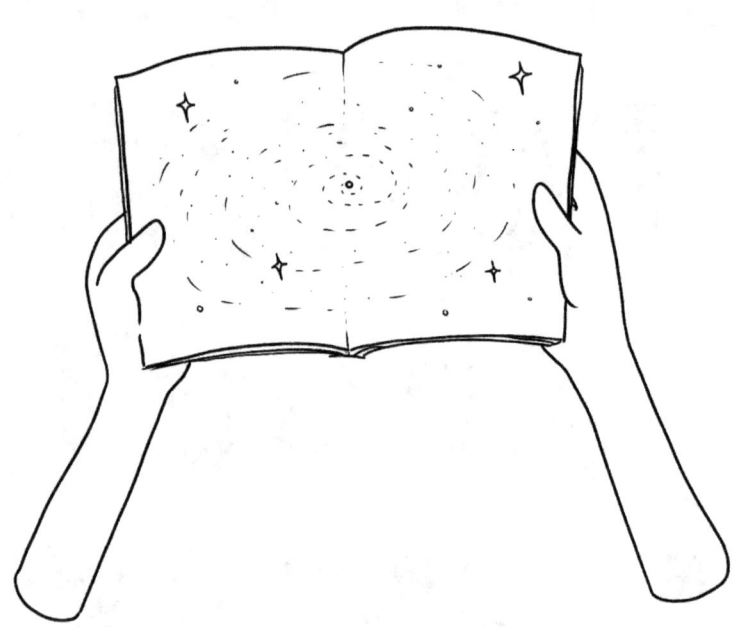

FOR ALL THOSE WHO READ,

This book is a compilation of journal entries, sketchbook pages, and notes app musings done throughout the course of 3 years. I've always wanted to write a book, and when I stopped obsessing over writing one, I just began writing instead. As it turns out, it's one of my favorite things in the world, and now I get to share this heart-centered work with the world. The drawings you'll see throughout are paired with certain writings in my journals or sketchbooks. I feel having the written and visual together are more powerful and give a greater understanding of the deeper meanings between the lines. Let the illustrations dance in your mind.

Even though I was born into the Christian church, I do not identify as a Christian. With that said, I reference Christian names and concepts as a default because they are the best ones I understand. There are infinite examples, stories, people, words, and explanations for what I am saying. Put your own aside for the time being and stay curious. During my teen years, I went through a long dark night of the soul, which is exactly what it sounds like. I retreated from the light, faith, and truth, to attempt to find it on my own while belonging to nothing.

This is where I have ended up after 10 years of rejecting God, exploring everything that lit me up, and accepting God back into my life. I have now gained a clear and deeper understanding of what ALL religions, cultures, faiths, and practices are saying at the heart of it.

From ancient Mesopotamia, ancient earth-based paganism, goddess worship, Buddhist meditation, Hinduism, Japanese Shintoism, ancient Egyptian sun and deity worship, the monotheist Jewish faith, gnostic Christianity, Catholics, indigenous communities all over the world, shamans, healers, witches, magicians, and alchemists— which you will see traces of throughout my work. We are all one humanity going through this human experience together. We are not separate, only by perception of form. Throughout the book, I play with the idea of duality— which will include language that will allude to a strict gender binary or black-and-white thinking. This is simply poetic and archetypal thinking, as I'm aware we all live and dance inside and outside of this binary of Light and Dark.

I am a student of life. I am dedicated to learning about what lights me up for the rest of my life, so I do not claim to be an expert on anything. Everything here comes from my experience, research, and inner knowing. I encourage you to see this book as a mirror for your own soul. Everything I am saying, you are just as capable of embodying and integrating yourself. Each piece of writing serves to expand your awareness even farther and deeper than you considered before...to ground in truth and rise in knowing— and as a gentle reminder of our shared humanity & divinity and the power of what Spirit can do if we allow ourselves to open up and receive the messages.

PREPARING FOR YOUR SPIRITUAL JOURNEY

Preparing for your spiritual journey is not talked about enough. The way media and people promote healing can become distorted because of the capitalistic and attachment-based lens society adheres to. True healing begins when we say "yes" and while the 'end result' (peace, love) obviously seems desirable, the 'result' is misleading. But, that's what this 'journey' is. You're embarking on your own hero's journey, as seen in mythology and modern media.

The hero's journey is for those who answer the call, go through hell, and make it through to the other side into heaven on earth. Heaven and hell are just polarized experiences we have on earth. Learning lessons about life, who you are, the truth your past holds, the deepest darkest parts of you, the sacrifices, loneliness, confusion, battles, and the cleansing of mind, body, and spirit. It is up to us to choose our own adventure and learn the truth about what life is all about and eventually, you feel the clarity of heart and peace you never thought possible, knowing you've gone through your own personal depths and can feel truly alive. This does not mean you never suffer, go through hardship, or experience loss and heartache again. But you are stronger than you were before. And you show up more prepared to face the next challenge, remembering all the times you didn't think you'd make it, and it turned out alright.

With love,
Megan

LIFE ON EARTH

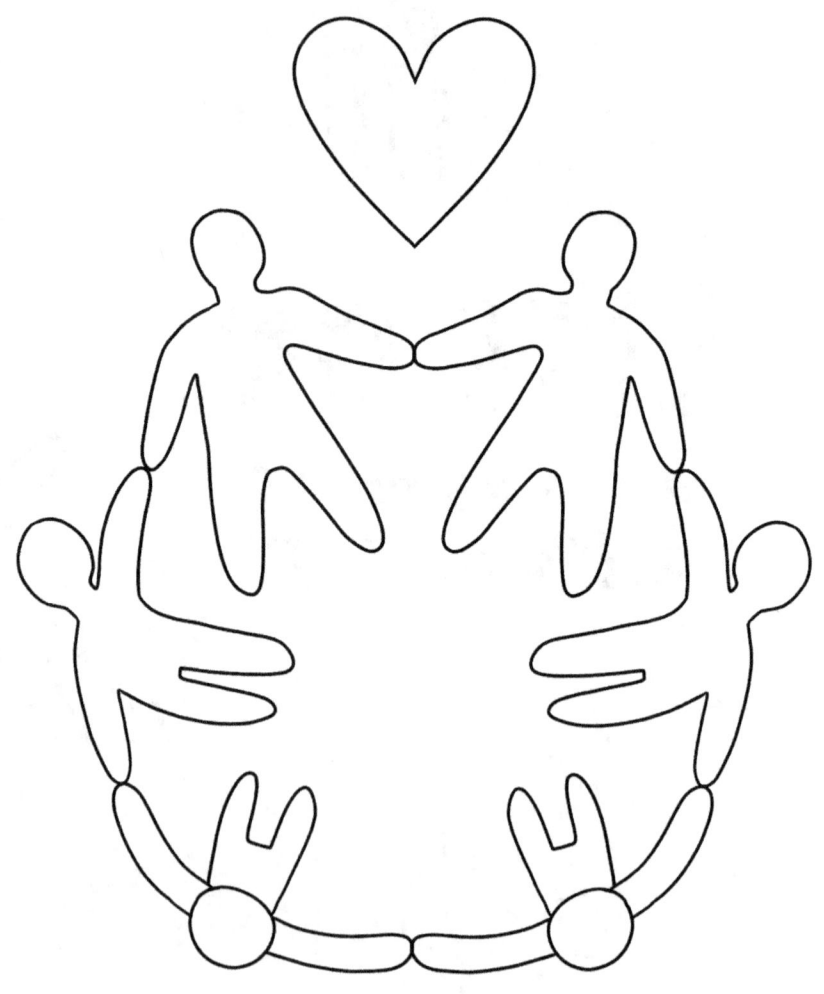

I LOVE YOU

You are not my child, but I want to say
I love you anyway
It doesn't matter if you're near or far
Or that you belong to another family
Because you are still family
We are all family...

I had a dream I was on top of a hill
Looking at the stars and feeling the earth
Holding me so still
I wept and knew the truth

Everything was a miracle
The mystery was love
The games disappeared
And we were one
And the same yet
Uniqueness in us all

From the dream, I awoke
Finally able to see by knowing
The truth was the same and it all was God
The spiral of the universe unfurling like a flower in infinite bloom

Death didn't scare me anymore
It was the same as any other moment

I found my home
My place
My belonging within the universe
All of the illusions dissolved and nothing mattered
In the most freeing and beautiful of ways
I glimpsed the Garden of Eden
The moment of infinite conception
Rebirth, death, life
Ego subsided
Earthly worries ceased

There was perfect harmony
And in the end

I was the all and the all was me.

THE MYTHS

Enslaved we are with outdated myths about life
Created by those who breathed long before today
What is a myth but a human-told story of how to be?

How to live?
What to believe?

Asleep to how each thought and action
Has been directed through generations,
And dare we ask, "Why?".

Those who claim to not believe in myths,
Are the very ones saturated in media, ancestral stories, and societal
expectations.

"We must live in a way that pleases the Gods."
The ancient ones whisper.

But in today's world, who are we living for?
CEO's
Politicians
Mother and Father
Or the fear-mongering man in the sky?

And with this, we embark on the hero's journey in service to
Abysmal falsehood
Valuing not love, not unity...
But our ego's idea of worthiness in the eyes of its gods.

Money, power, control
All self-serving nonsense
For the benefit of "I"
Not us
For the sake of a life of fleeting emptiness
Void of progress and improvement
Leaving the planet no different than you left it
With the gold-laden dust
Of who you once were.

But, if you choose to decide who you live for
With love in your heart
You can create a new way to be,

Regenerative
Fulfilling
Overflowing with service to this mysterious life
And all those who share it with you

Remember, you are the hero of your own story

If you choose to believe it.

ZOOM IN

ZOOM OUT

I am not the first to arrive
Many have before
And more will come after

Zoom in
Zoom out

On earth, we are here
Consciousness all around
Zoom in, observe the hidden
Zoom out, perceive the unknown

Life always seems to find its way
Through the impossible
Proving that perceived obstacles
Are but illusions.

Complexity of life is not limited by design
Nor should you underestimate
A seemingly simple organism
It contains multitudes

We are all programmed to do
Exactly what we're supposed to
Turning singular information
Into complex form, and effortless intelligence.

The journey of life on earth
Involves steep climbs
Cuts and bruises
Obstacles that conceal
Death, decay, destruction
Yet birth, bursting bright.

Climb until you realize
The goal is nowhere to be found
Only perceived...

THE TOP OF THE MOUNTAIN
WILL ALWAYS BE HERE.

Born into a culture
Stripped at birth
Naked and clothed
By systems that
Rob humans of
Their birthrights
Until much later
Then we discover
What is pulling
The strings
And thinking the thoughts
That move us
And we choose
To die in life
Or die in death
And you know what?
It's not mom and dad's fault
Mom and dad
Are victims of the system too
They did their best
With what they knew
At the time
Likely not knowing
Themselves in the process
Innocent are we all
Pawns on a chess board
Until we reach
The other side
And become our own
Kings and queens
All the mothers
The fathers
The daughters and sons
All the children
Of this earth
Holy as we come

Worn down as we go
A sick society
A sick world
Who's to blame?
Hurt people
Hurt people
Who hurt people
Power rises
Power falls
Not for the good
Of all
Power does not belong
In the hands
Of hurt people
Who hurt people
But with lovers
Who rule with compassion
A helping hand
And a forgiving heart
Arms spread open
Ready to hold
Where are the lovers?
They are all around
With little love
To give themselves
But with a little help
We can learn to love
The parts of us
We've learned to hate
And take a stand for
What's right
What's true
And little by little
The world can heal
Together.

When one falls into depression in today's modern world...
We give them pills, talk therapy, and sterile treatments masked as a cure.

We do not ask when or why you stopped

Laughing
Playing
Dancing
Singing
Expressing

Depression has become so normalized
We have begun to blame the individual
And yet we do not criticize

The environment
The society
The structures
The patterns
The oppression

That in fact trigger a deep-rest.

What is depression other than a hibernation from the world?

The more conscious I become

The more I become attuned to the fleetingness

Of life, form, and experiences

It is all so precious and should never be taken for granted

Hugs become tighter

Touch becomes gold

Experiences become priceless memories

Tears become sacred reminders of a life full of love

Thank you.

Thank you.

Thank you.

Thank you.

I cracked myself open again today

All that's been fermenting has spilled
And pooled
And flooded the ground

It's been years since this has been bottled
And put to rest in the cellar

I cannot remember
The last time I cried over the impermanence of life
And how when left exposed
There is only
Love
Beauty
Grace
Behind all of that pain
And shards of glass
Meant to keep safe

I am drunk on the Truth once again
In hysterics, and marveling
Knees to the floor
Eyes closed in realization
With the bottle on the ground
And tears in my palms
I wipe away the distortion
That has kept me sober for far too long

DOUBLE LIFE

Off in heaven on earth
Dancing with light and
Living in love

How does one integrate
This double life?

Each day is mundane, yet a miracle

This paradoxical existence
The duality of the physical world
The spirit world
It perplexes me

We see no division
Yet there is separation.

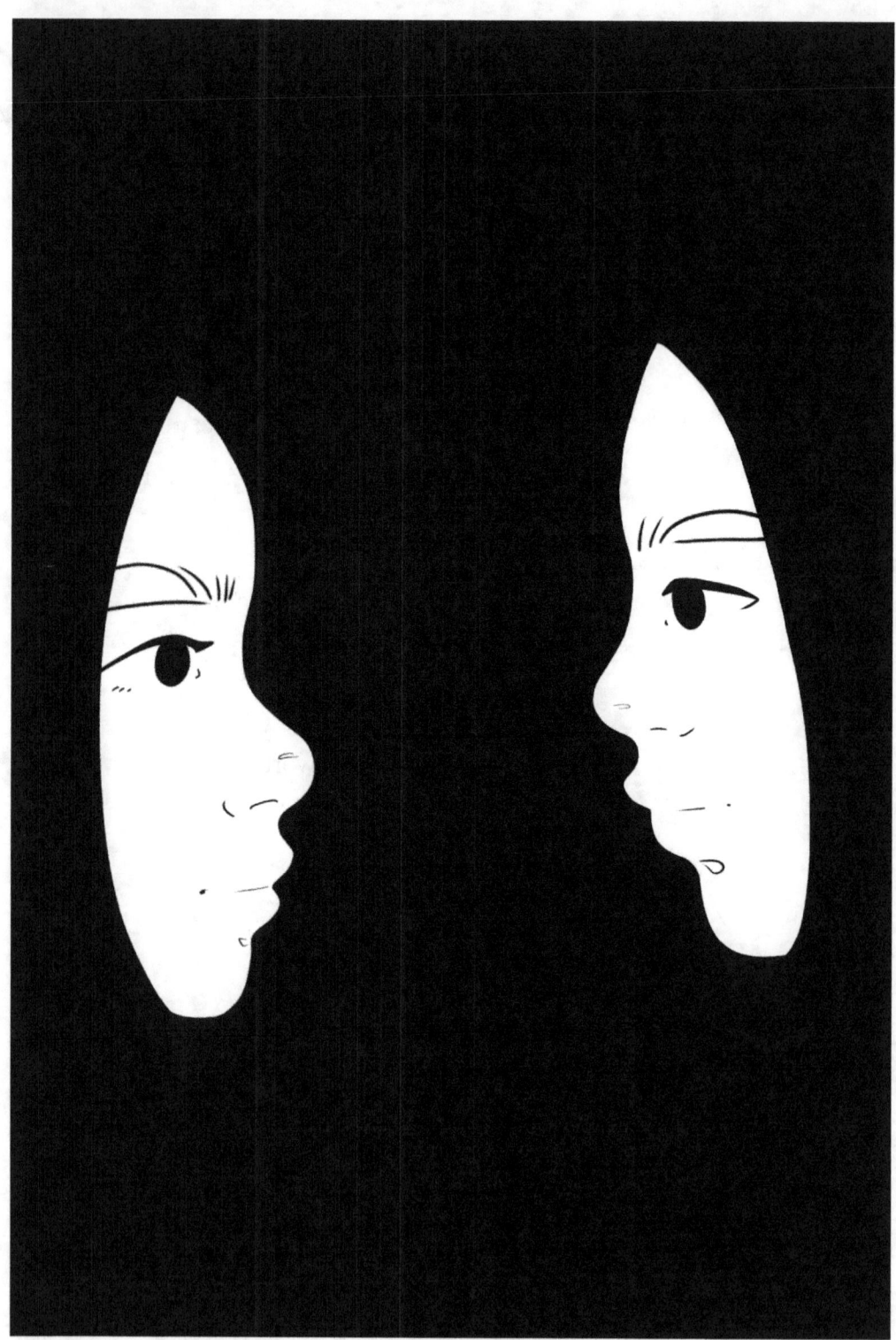

FACES

We are all around each other
At one moment or the next, a face reflected by your own
Eyes, ears, mouth, body, essence, consciousness

We walk alongside, behind, separate from each other or hand in hand
I could never see your face again, yet we are two cosmic vessels
coming into contact with each other's senses...
Staring, wondering, observing, sharing space

We take one look, maybe four, wondering about the other

What kind of day are you having? What do you like?

And sometimes, I walk the other way, avoiding gazes
Pretending like you and I are invisible
For some sense of safety?
Not wanting to be known?
Not wanting to be near anyone at all
Yet yearning and aching for them all

We know the faces we call home, but can we all come home to each
other?

We are one even if we try and fight to not see
The magic of two universes
Colliding, creating and transforming

Life and consciousness into a new living thing
A new vessel
A new face.

FATHER SUN

The sun says good morning to you each day
Do you say it back?
Do you look at the sun with gratitude and thanks for rising yet again?

Infinite, eternal, cyclical

Do you give thanks for the sun?
For giving you life? Light?
A new opportunity to grow and change every day?

Even when the sun is hidden
Or you feel like it's not there
Do you forget that it still rises?
It never went away
It did not leave you or abandon you
It loves you unconditionally
The sun does not forget you though you may not see it even on the
stormiest days
He still shows up
On cloudless days
Gray days
Summer days
And the cold winter ones too...

He who gives us life,
Loves us eternally.

EARTH MOTHER

The earth holds you, and never lets go.
Do you forget the embrace of the earth?
Do you kiss the earth with gratitude and thanks for holding you no
matter what?
Infinite, eternal, present
Do you give thanks for the earth?
For giving you shelter
Food
Water
Endless possibilities of
Abundance
Hands to hold
Constant support?
Even when you feel in constant motion
Or the world won't stop spinning
Do you forget your feet on the ground?
It never went away
It never left you
It loves you unconditionally
The earth does not forget you
You may not feel it
Even in the harshest of events
She still prevails
In lush forests, mountains, rivers and streams
Volcanoes, grassland, and tundra
On the days when everything is
Vibrant, green, alive
And on the days when everything is in decay

She who births us, loves us eternally.

MY MOTHER TOLD ME

About a time
When I was a child
I asked her,
"Mommy, why does Auntie look different?"
And my mother takes out
Two eggs
One brown, one white
Then, she cracks them
And asks me which is which
I could not tell her
And, I understood.

WE LEARN CLOSEST TO OUR SUN

Certain lessons about life on earth
Specific messages we've learned to receive
And what about the other suns?
Those stars in the sky?
Can we learn from them too?
What would they have to say if we listened?
Father sun, are there others like you?

ALL THE BEINGS IN THE UNIVERSE

Creating heaven all around
Yet we still fight
And can't get along....
When we get better
The earth gets better
She keeps giving back
Even though we've strayed
Far away from the ancient ways
The best thing that can be done
Is to use your voice
And weave love
Into leadership

ALL LIFE ON EARTH WAS BORN
FROM THE WATERS

Therefore nothing separates us from it
Isn't it beautiful that
Since the waters have granted us this opportunity of consciousness
We, in return, have to drink from that same source to stay alive?
All living beings are given this gift
And we all find a way to keep the balance
Of give and take
As creatures of the waters
So separated from our source
The least we can do
Is preserve the eternal fountain
Of what keeps us here.

WE MUST SHAKE UP THE WAY THINGS ARE

In order to create space for new growth
Like springtime on earth
We can learn to rebirth
Infinitely, cyclically
Plant new seeds
Ideas, plans, visions, projects, passions, mindsets
Values, opportunities, experiences, and lessons
Giving back to the earth

Time and time again.

THOSE WHO DARE

To speak their truth
In the name of love
Become torches in the night
Altering everyone around them
Because suddenly there's fire
A flame burning too bright

Humanity is enslaving itself
Not God, not Jesus

Oppression creates pressure
And over time, things collapse
If we took a step back
And let it fall down

Could we rebuild a new world?
The one God wants for its Children?
Jesus loves you
The church doesn't

Jesus loves you
The patriarchy doesn't

Jesus loves you
But we're still mad at him, because we're at war with ourselves
And can't see the real structures set in place.

We humans have overlooked our experience of the universe

For eternal suffering instead of eternal life.
The point is to merge the oneness granted after you die
Into your eternal now moment
Consciously
We are here to play and enjoy god's creation
To its fullest and highest form
Because that is what has been gifted to us!

But we as humans have forgotten this ancient truth of unity and love

This is why remembering is the pathway to liberation from suffering.

the less I define myself,
the more available I am
to other human beings.
the less I am living within
the box of my self definition,
that constantly uses the
universe to reassure me
of who I am.

Ram Dass

I wonder if I close my eyes
What I can learn from the allness of everything

To feel that wisdom
Permeating each cell of my body

To recognize the infinite
In each shade of grey
Dancing in the rainbow of consciousness
Questioning
A new way of being

What's it like to be a tree?
Or a fox?
Or a bee?

To view the world
From the eyes of a sparrow
Flying high above the sea?

What's it like to be the ocean?
Pulsing, crashing
Immortal and unwavering?

To be sight, sound, taste, touch, smell?

What is it like…to exist in a new vision of reality?

Where the allness of everything
Is the alleness of me.

To express oneself is the greatest breakthrough a human can make

Here is something to do more than simply survive...
More than just existing...

There is an infinite rainbow of ways to weave
Love into our lives
And show each other

That trick of the light.

We think we are a superior, advanced, intelligent species
Because we invent and build innovative technologies
and manipulate the earth, bending it to our will.

Yet, living together in love is far-fetched

Getting along with each other is virtually impossible

Caring for the earth is pointless

What kind of advanced species are we if we cannot transcend
ego-driven, selfish, temporary & material motives?

Why can't we innovate from a place of universal harmony and
well-being for the earth and all its inhabitants?

THE SPIRAL

DUALITY

An eternal dance of creation

One can not exist without the other

Sun and Moon
Life and Death
Heaven and Hell
Man and Woman
Light and Dark

Creating something new
With each step

Birthing new worlds
With every embrace

Push, pull
In a trance

Weaving threads of time and space
The physical and invisible

This cosmic duality dances together
And from union
Comes creation.

DEATH & REBIRTH

The never ending spiral
With change comes immense up-leveling
And time is needed to integrate this new energy

In these in between periods of rapid rebirth cycles
Everything feels chaotic, ungrounded, egotistic, and fear based
And brings up many shadows for us to face

This is normal and needed
This is all a part of the infinite unfolding of the universe

"God's plan."

Ultimately, we come down back into God's arms and rest with a
newer, clearer, sense of safety and Love.

So those chaotic places we get caught up in,
Those loops that just won't stop
They are there for you to cut the cords of that cycle
They are there so you can move on, move higher
Cleanse your being of old, negative, heavy, dense energy that is only
Bringing you down vibrationally

Sometimes they feel like the dragon inside of you
That the hero needs to slay
Sometimes they feel like your 8 year old self screaming
Crying asking for your attention

Sometimes it feels like fog, or like there's no light at the end of the
tunnel, like each foot forward is all you can see.

Since each foot forward is all you have
You can decide

Which direction you would like to walk in and begin walking there
Accepting that challenges will come with it,
Anticipated or not
And being prepared to do anything to keep heading in that direction
Step by step.

Eventually, you can see your path
Because you're walking it
And enjoying the view
And realizing that you faced all of those challenges and made it out
alive, and smiling!
You can feel the sun on your soul
Because you know where to go
No matter what
God doesn't give up on you
Though you may have given up on God

This is why faith is so powerful

Because sometimes we think
Hey, I've been here before, and things always changed for the better

So why don't I keep walking
Day by day
Remember to believe
Day by day
So you may truly
Walk with God
And never be alone in each death again.

THE CAVE IS CALLING

A thunderous sky
Echoes within my mind
I have let the light speak
And now I give darkness
Room to grow
To ebb and flow without resistance
Is to honor the gift of life.

GROWING MAY FEEL LIKE...

Breaking at first...
Like wild weeds cracking concrete
Old structures once built to
Protect, sustain, preserve
The life which lies within
No longer inhabited by
Its old residents
The owner is a ghost
Living within the walls
That took
Blood, sweat, tears
To erect
The ghost dissipates
With each crack
Vine
Weed
Dandelion
Until the walls begin
To crumble
And the ghost
Can finally rest
Now that there's
Room to grow.

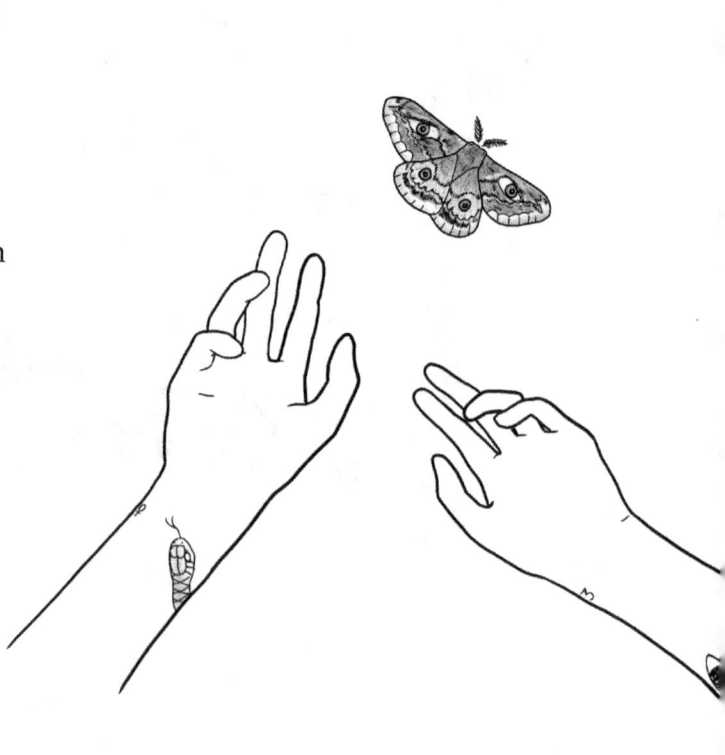

...REBIRTH.

Give way for new life
New sight
I see the subtleties
In a blade of grass
Under the born again sun
Wildflowers cracking open
After a dense and claustrophobic
Time underground.

The light of day touches us
Revealing our true nature

Rainbows appear
Where skin and hair once were

Realizations once shrouded in a darkness
Unforgiving shoot up through the dirt
And bloom within my consciousness

A thousand "oo's" and "ahh's" permeate
My being
It all makes sense
It always did
And it always will
So long as the wheel still turns
And spring erupts with life.

WITNESSING YOUR OWN DEATH

Your decay into new life
Mourning, grieving, confusion, apathy, fatigue
We must ALL move through these energies in relation to our own
evolution and development.

The new life, way of being, or paradigm is there. It always has been.
What we can not avoid though is loss and grief of the old. It does
not mean that you are losing yourself, getting worse, regressing, or
anything that feels dense or stressful.

It just means you are passing through the shadows, the valley of
death, and coming face to face with everything that comes with it.

The journey through the valley is not permanent, though it is entire-
ly necessary in one's life path. It's a tale as old as time. Life, death,
rebirth.

How can we come to terms with this fundamental truth?

It comes down to how you walk it.
Do you cower in fear?
Hide for days in darkness?
Freeze under pressure?
Or do you move with courage?

Embrace each obstacle as a vital lesson, and challenge it with a
smile?

Walk like a warrior, ready for every single moment?
That choice is yours

Either way, you will make it to the other side
You just get to decide how you do it
The way is long, ever-unfolding, never-ending
There is something at the end, the perceived one, the place we're all going

The way must not be approached by expecting shortcuts, loopholes
Better yet, total bypassing of the way itself
There are no shortcuts, only death

What we are all seeking is not anything of this earth
It is the infinite light that embraces us upon passing
Reunification of the soul and the one

The truth is not found, it is
The truth is not tangible, found in ancient tomes or tombs
It is the eternal now
The force inside all life
The intelligence of the cosmos
The love found between eye contact
The mysterious unraveling of everything

It is here
There is no seeking
Only being here now
In love with life.

SPRING PUSHES THROUGH

Life force awakens
And forces its way
Through the hard dirt
Cracking through the density
Of all the life that once was
Now, beneath the surface
Ready to become
Something new

My breath deepens
My rib cage expanding
My stomach fills with butterflies
My heart surging with electricity

Something new is moving through me
Pregnant with life
But not with child
My being begs to
Release
Surrender
And allow
The birth of
Something new

Deep within me
Lies the beginning

Layer by layer
I revoke each shell

Like a Russian doll
Each face begins anew

LIVING IN YOUR OWN SHADOW

The constant reminder
Of who you once were
Who you had in your life
And knowing
It's gone forever
The past escapes me
Yet shows itself
In the corner
Of my eyes
Grieving the body
Mind
Heart
That which does not exist
Yet stays the same

These pieces of me
Given away so effortlessly
Never to be returned
The mourning process
Hurts profoundly more
When you've buried it all away
And comes back
As zombies and ghosts
Knocking on the door of my heart

I can't keep the door locked anymore
It's wide open now
Meeting and confronting

The beings I've buried underground
Locked away in the grounds
Of the garden of my heart
Little by little
The skeletons turn to flesh and blood
The hosts release into the eternal
Greeting them and sending them off
After having tea over tears
The hardest part
Is shutting the door behind them
It's a different kind of loss
Aware of what you've realized
Releasing attachments
Connections
Love, tears, time spent together

I'm grateful for it all
Now I sit in silence, now that they're gone
Drinking in new life through dried tears
My power, slowly returns.

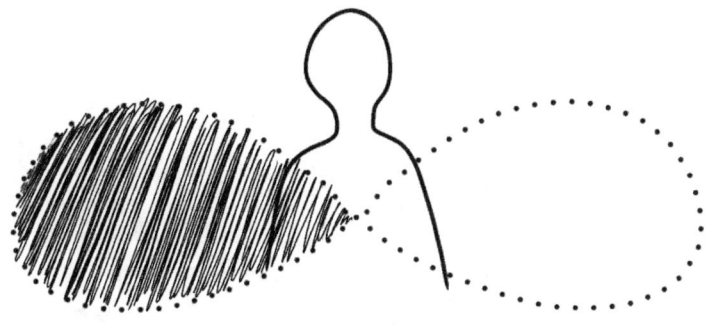

IF GOD IS LIGHT...

WHY DO WE CHASE
OUR SHADOWS?

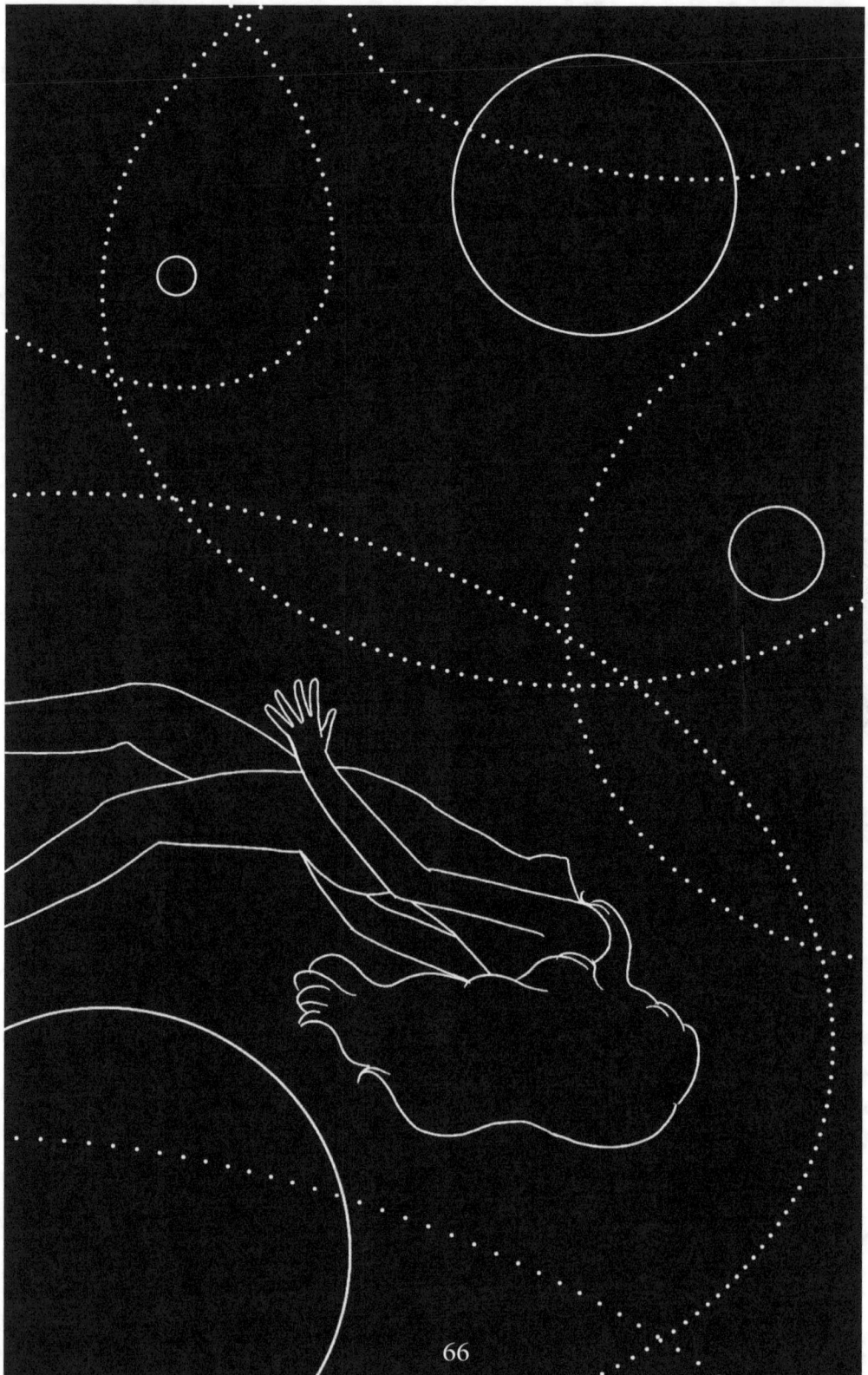

The infinite intelligence is still
Weaving endlessly as we speak
We are of a shared thread
In the fabric of space and time
The duality that dances together

And creates from unity.

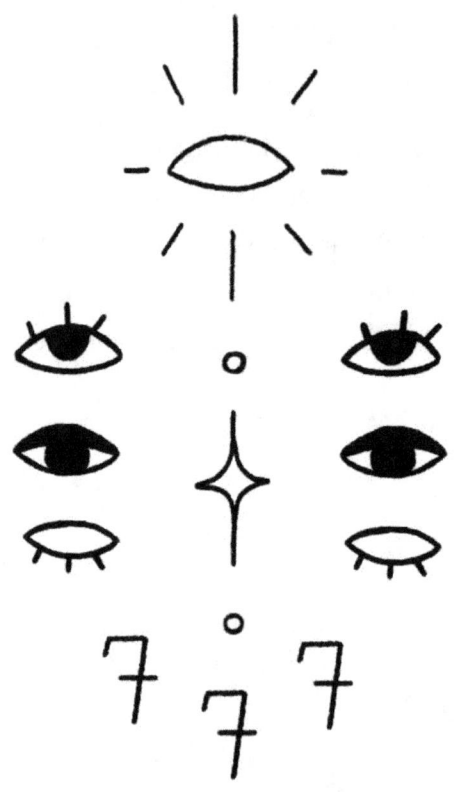

AKASHA

What is the inner world?

TRUE BEING

Exists outside of form
It lives in the eternal now of pure consciousness
The world of form is a playground
For consciousness to explore itself.

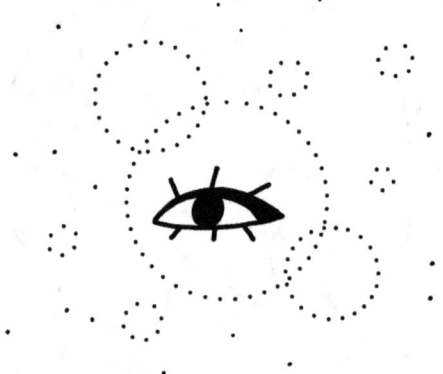

BEHIND THE VEIL OF YOUR EYELIDS

Exists a space that is full of infinite wisdom
Depending on your relationship with that space
You may know
Truth, love, peace, and stillness within
When you return to the dimension of form
You can bring this deep knowing wherever you go
For it never truly left you
As long as you create more space within and
Connect with yourself
You realize you are never alone.

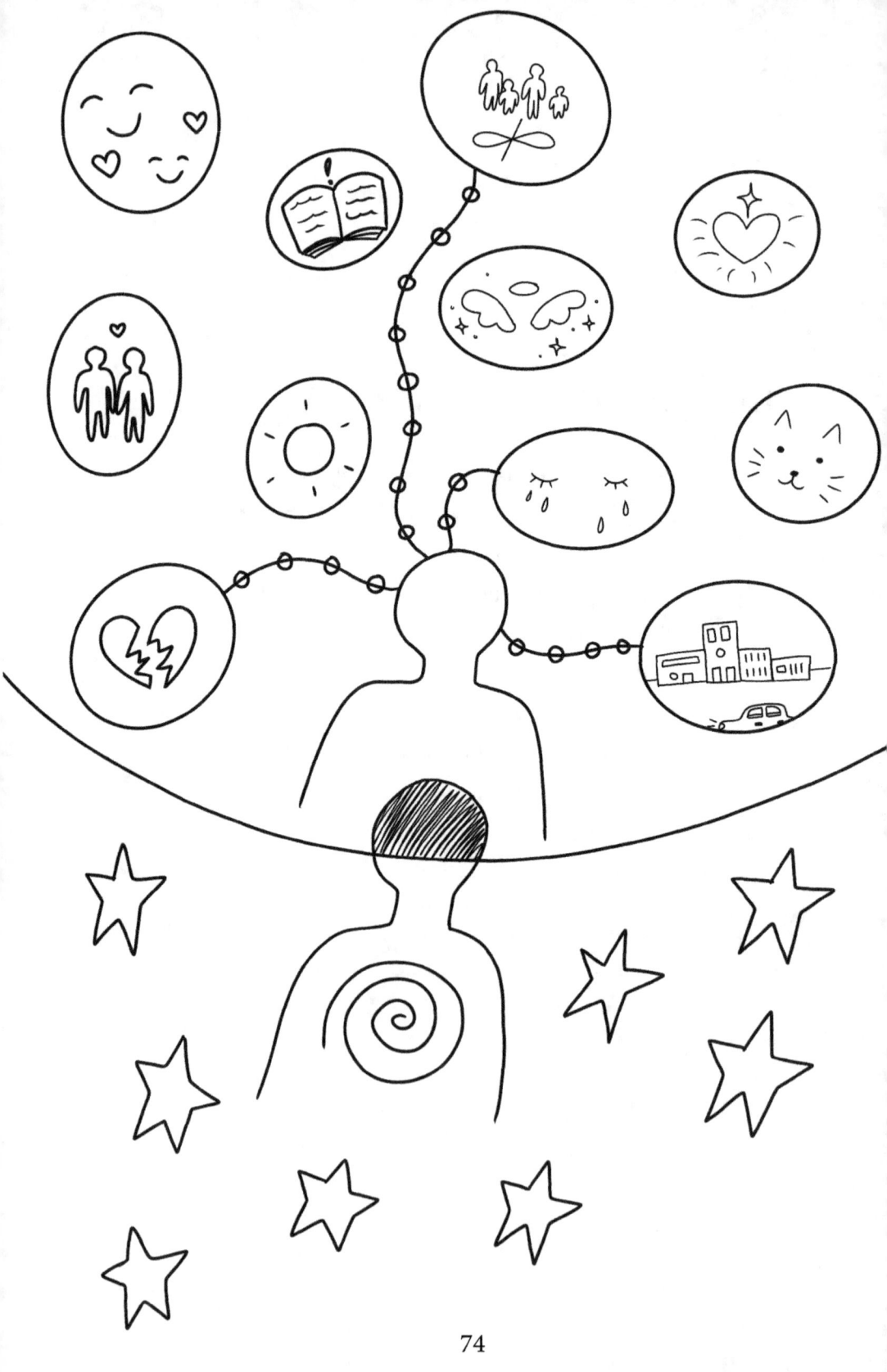

HERE AND NOW

Memories, projections, dreams, imagination, experiences, traumas
Emotions, thoughts, stories, people, places, things, feelings

These do not exist in the here and now
Only in the mind are they kept alive by careful analysis
The magic is here, all around you, for infinity inwards and outwards

Break the chains.

MOST OF OUR LIVES

We operate from the subconscious mind
Everything we experienced as a child when we were not fully
conscious.

And everything we store that we don't want to deal with
Is how we move through each day

Until we die

Unless, however
You begin to take a step back from yourself
Observe the patterns
Setbacks
Fears
Resistance
Read the story of ourselves and learn from the world
And then, begin to rewrite our lives

Into the most beautiful
Expansive
Wise
Loving
And abundant timeline.

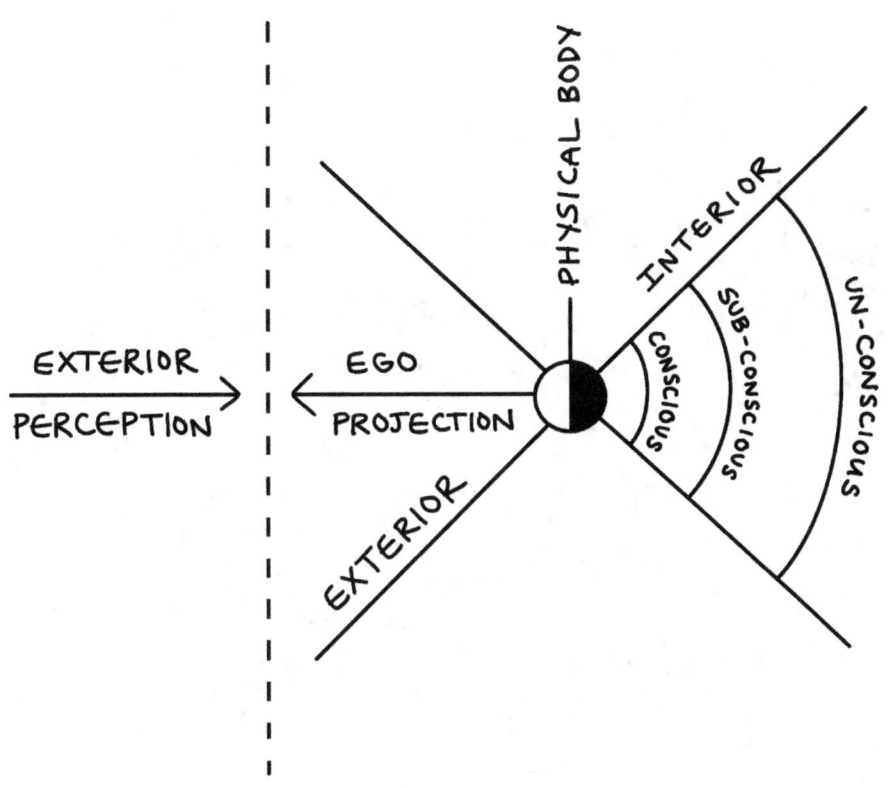

THE GARDEN OF EDEN

Deep inside of me lies a place only the myths and mystics speak of
A place that can only be found in stillness and quiet contemplation
Where heaven and earth converge
Where the dust of yesterday and the mist of tomorrow commune
with me.
Where two become one: The Garden of Eden.
A place not sought for, but found
A place where man and God can be together in secret
Only meeting briefly; for if there was to be a moment longer
Man would never return to their earthly home
This place, both within and without
Infinite and fleeting
May never be discovered by most men
The mystics are a dying breed and cannot live to tell the way
Which is why
The whole of the world must rest and go within
It is often a treacherous journey for most
Most men seek the garden in places they'll never find it
Mystics like I have glimpsed the garden…
Even rested beneath the trees…
The stillness requires curiosity
Which tends to be severed after if not during childhood
The mystics are the children
The men who have not forgotten
The women who remembered
The mystics will rise and walk everyone home within themselves
A perfect meeting.

Your permanent place of residence lies within.

Is it always peaceful, safe, fun, clean, bright, loving, supportive
Unshakable, calm, filled with laughter and abundance

You live here, and nothing can ever change that

When everything feels out of control, scary, unsafe, or negative,
We can return home to this place inside

And then you recognize and remember this feeling and
Take it with you.

It doesn't matter what or who shows up at your door
Thank them for coming by

And, depending on who's there, you choose to talk to, let in, or say
no. Choose to share the love you feel within with everything you
come into contact with.

Because you know where you live, too.

You have traveled to many places. There is no doubt the terror and
darkness that forever lurks.

You learn from your experiences, question yourself over and over
again

Until, you've seen enough and
It's time to come home.

Turn yourself
Upside down

Enlighten
The hidden places
Too scared
To be seen

Become
The observer
And choose
A loving perspective
Rather than one
Of fear

Accept it all
For what it is
And not what you
Make it to be

Walk out
Of the mind
Drop down
To the heart
Lighten your load
Let it all fall
To the ground

Allow
Allow
Allow...

...The light
To show the way.

You must rewrite your past from a higher and loving perspective to get different results in the present and future.

Stop playing the victim

Start seeing from a new perspective and stop replaying the same Stories about yourself and reality that no longer serve your highest good.

We are able to experience new realities at any moment if we allow ourselves to leave the current one.

If we can tell new stories to ourselves, we end up reprogramming our minds to shift our perspective...

Thus creating a new reality.

When all feels like
It's crumbling to the ground
When people's tongues go sharp and you can't escape yourself
When you feel small, hopeless, down on yourself
No matter the ailment
This is when you pray

And keep praying

Prayer is the lamplight for the soul on it's path through the unknown.

Prayer is our bridge to divine liberation
To Higher connection, clarity, strength, and love

It is a pure surrender

We can not do this alone

Prayer is what helps us remember.

Another day, I am alive
Another day, to feel
Every morning, God's gift
In mourning, I wake
Remembering every feeling unfelt
Through years and years and years
Of beauty, and death
The death of old
Each falling leaf
Each falling petal
Given back to the earth
Again and again
Each tear, nourishment for my soul
To grow and grow and become more
To grow more into myself each day
And to mourn each morning
The death of who I used to be
And what is to come
I am learning to feel again
Not just in mind but in body
And I mourn the days
The weeks
The months
The years
That I've forgotten
That I flew away within myself
Somewhere far away
And forgot all of this beautiful magic
That's part of being alive each day
Maybe its heaven, maybe it's hell

But what if it's both?
But God, it's so beautiful
This mystery, I call home for now
This body I carry with me
And love so tenderly
Even when I forget
Again and again and again
And through these tears
I weave connection back
Through each and every one of us
I remember this
That I am not alone in this lifetime or the next
And that I will mourn this life
In heaven
And pray to god to give me another chance
At life on earth again.

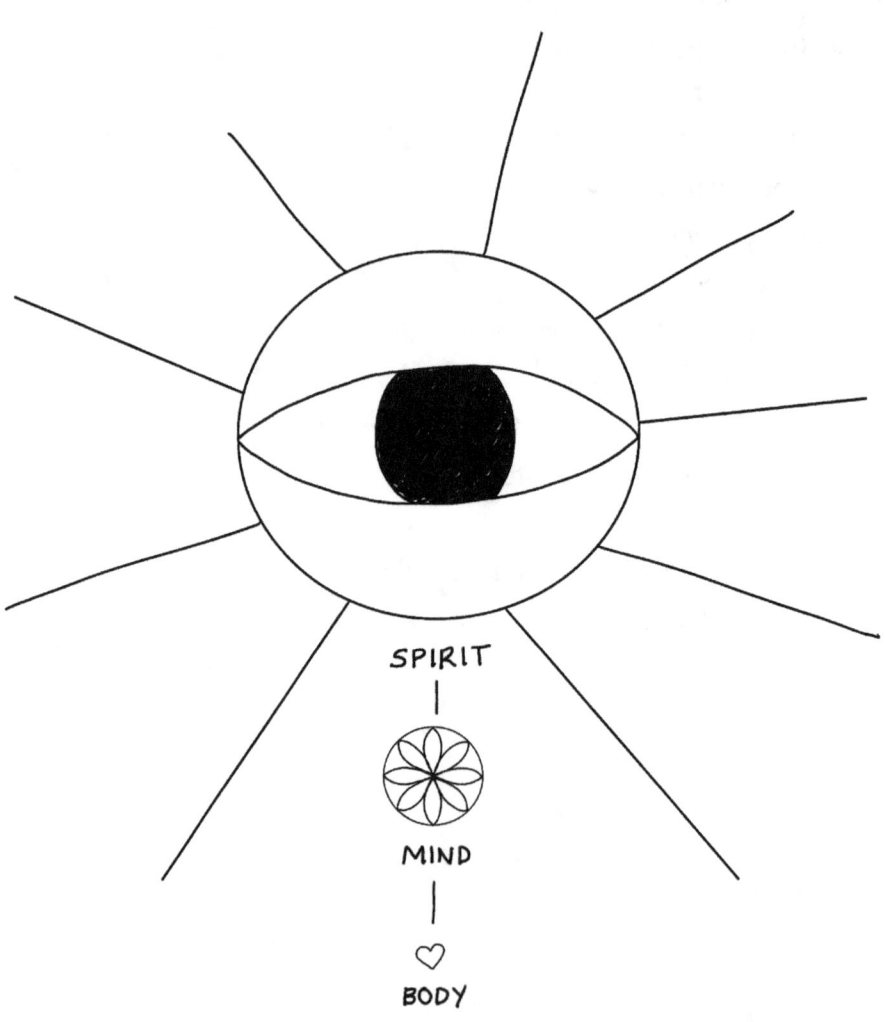

SPIRIT

MIND

BODY

GOD IS LOVE

Don't isolate when you have God's arms wide open for you.

Build the bridge.

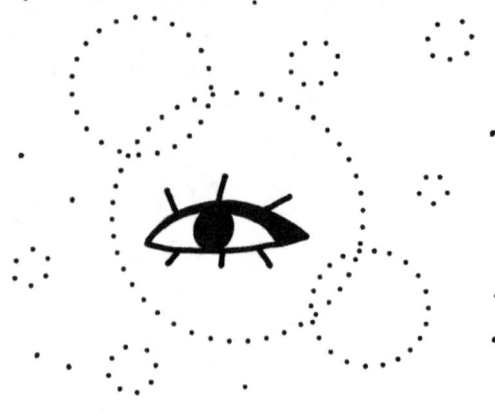

If we go back in time
To the beginning
There was a big bang
A burst of light
An infinitely intelligent singularity
Let out a long sigh
And suddenly here we are
I don't know about you
But that sounds alot like God to me.

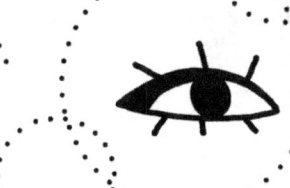

God is love
Love is a feeling
Love is patient, love is kind
Not violence, nor fear
Love is oneness
In the here and now
Together
Not me and you, but us.

I am the unsinkable ship
No matter the strife
I remain
No matter the storm
I remain
No matter the situation
I am always intact

I will always keep you safe
I will always guide you through the waters
The stars, as my sign posts

The moons turning phases,
The rush of wind that directs my sail

I am always here, in total perfection

Carrying you, shore to shore
And through the path

Within and without.

With our heightened awareness and perception via consciousness, we are all able to get impressions of God within us.

If we close our eyes and imagine what the feelings of love, peace, forgiveness, patience, safety, and kindness *feel like* in the body and notice the sensation, we are sensing God.

Subtle vibrations throughout your whole body, a warm honey-like sun, an unimaginable light, the body of a river with crystal clear waters.

When we begin to develop this awareness of our own body's energy, we can expand it into objects we hold, people we meet, places that spark the soul. Only if we allow our mind to take a back seat.
When we close our eyes, we cannot see, only sensing what is beyond sight itself.

We gaze into nothingness, and become it
And in this nothingness, there is truth
Not what you momma told you
Not what your teacher said
Not what your best friend thinks
Or what your culture says

But what infinitely and perfectly IS.

THERE IS NO RIGHT RELIGION

No #1 group, race, culture...
To assume oneself at the top of a hierarchy in relation to faith is playing God.

We ourselves are not "right" by being christian, Muslim, Jewish, an atheist, a Buddhist, whatever

To impose correctness is to miss the point
The only true, powerful authority of love and creation is God

Not the people who feed their spiritual ego with fearful power and authority over others.

The love I feel
For life on earth
Does not belong to me
This love is borrowed

For though the human capacity
To love is limited
Therein lies a Source
Much greater than
The sum of a simple creature

When I look at the spirals of the universe
Sprinkled throughout the land
It is not me at all who admires these creations

It is something far more ancient
Beyond this mind's comprehension

This body is God's looking glass
Made to adore all she has birthed into the world

For this otherworldly feeling that consumes me
And fills this body to the brim
Is the love of the Mother of All Life
Gazing at her children

When was the last time you cracked your own heart open?
Surrendered to it all?

Fear, grief, miracles and life
Breathing into the shadowy depths
And sinking within pools of liquid light
Spilling through the cracks

What a relief, to remember!
Once, twice, until I die!

The days spin on
Not a prayer in mind
Until I feel my heartbeat
Knocking at the door

Tender and warm
The feeling familiar yet glorious
Brimming with joy
Met with a gaze from
Newborn eyes and an ancient soul
Already knowing
I'd arrive here again today.

Words fail when giving voice to God's True Nature

The truth is, there will never be the right way to tell the world

What lies between the fabric of this otherworldly existence

But, if chosen carefully

There might be time

To read between the lines

And discover a certain type of prayer

Living in the silence.

God can be found anywhere, at any time.

The wind between the shifting trees
The echo of a baby's laughter
The teardrop which transforms pain into bliss

Your call, is God's answer

I AM

Constantly getting to know myself
My whole life is remembering and honoring my energy as
it unfolds before my own eyes
Unconditionally.

The human drama is simple
The world's a stage
We're putting on costumes
People are suffering
And we care more about our scene
Than the hungry people in the crowd

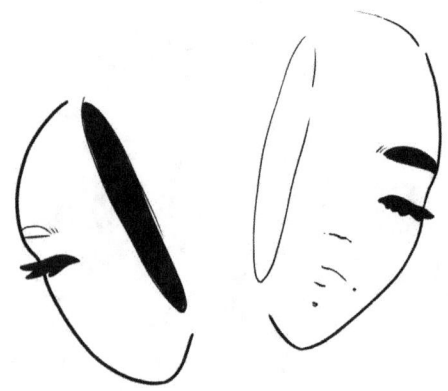

When the mind tells you to give up
The heart beats and whispers,
"Keep going."

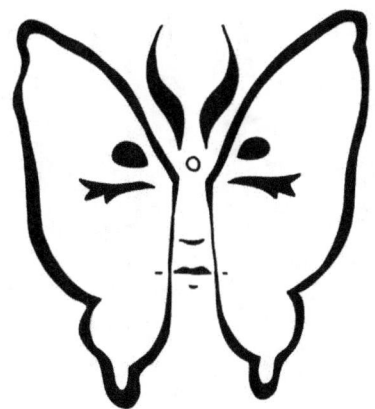

Some days
I am the sun
My light is
Blinding and warm.

Some days
I am the storm
My inner presence
Tumultuous.

Some days
I am the clear sky
My energy bright
And expansive.

Some days
I am everything
And nothing at all.

And everyday
I am still alive
No matter
The weather.

No matter how lonely I feel

I know deep down that I am one with the world and I walk with
The universe hand in hand
Each person, place, animal, plant, element, particle
I choose to remember the divinity of this miracle and to dance
With the allness of infinity of each now moment

And so it is.

I am a flower of the earth
A culmination of intelligence
Sourced long ago
Born to be
And rise
To meet the sun
Born to infinitely unfold
Before the world
With fierce vulnerability
And an open heart

And so it is.

With the light of our awareness, we gain clarity and knowing that gifts us with all that has been buried and hidden beneath the surface.

When everything comes up to be seen and loved

Then, we can dance
In our
Uniqueness
Magic

And the radiant truth of who we are.

I am the shapeshifter
Born to explore multitudes

A kaleidoscope of awareness
Beholding infinity in one form

Rising from the black earth
Into the white light of the sun

A spectrum of experiences
Coloring the dance of life.

GIVING UP.

SURRENDERING.

I CAN'T KEEP LIVING LIKE THIS.

GOD, PLEASE HELP ME.

I AM AT YOUR MERCY.

I AM LOST, GOD.

PLEASE GUIDE ME.

I AM BLIND, GOD.

PLEASE HELP ME TO SEE.

I AM DEAF, GOD.

PLEASE HELP ME TO LISTEN.

I AM HUNGRY, GOD, PLEASE FEED ME.

I AM WOUNDED, GOD, PLEASE HEAL ME.

I AM MUTE, GOD.

HELP ME TO SPEAK.

I AM WROUGHT WITH PETTY THOUGHTS, GOD.

PLEASE HELP ME TO THINK CLEARLY.

I AM SCARED, GOD, PLEASE PROTECT ME.

I AM HURT, GOD, PLEASE CARE FOR ME.

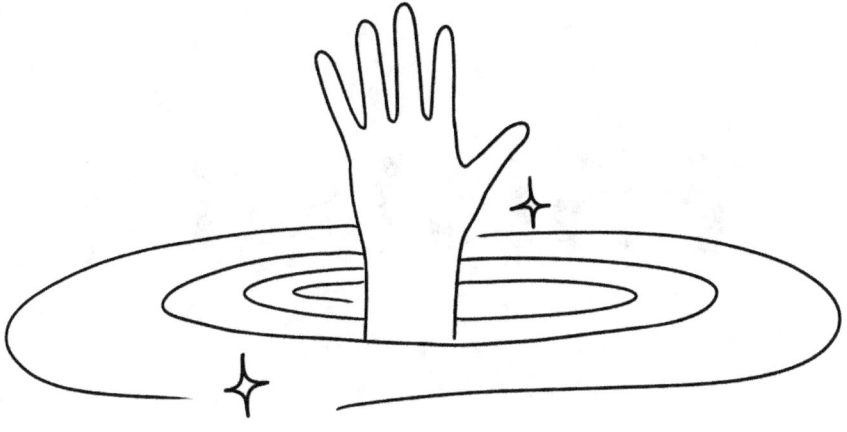

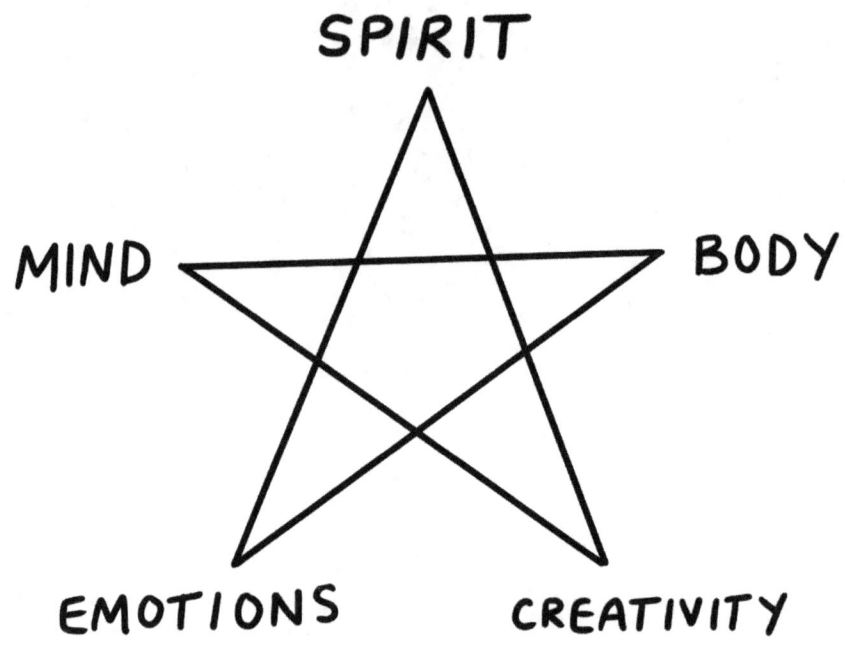

BALANCE

I am fully cutting old cords that only tie me down
I release old ways of being that do not serve my highest good
I release judgment I cast upon myself and others
I release memories of people and experiences
That keep me in a victim mentality
I release subconscious and unconscious ties with people who do not
Add light into my field
Internally and externally
I release outdated expectations I or others may have encoded
Into my being
I allow Higher Love
Grace
Wisdom
Purity
Kindness
Generosity
Abundance
Strength
Inspiration
Creativity
Collaboration
Partnerships
And timelines that all resonate to the highest frequency
Of my soul's path.

AND SO

IT IS.

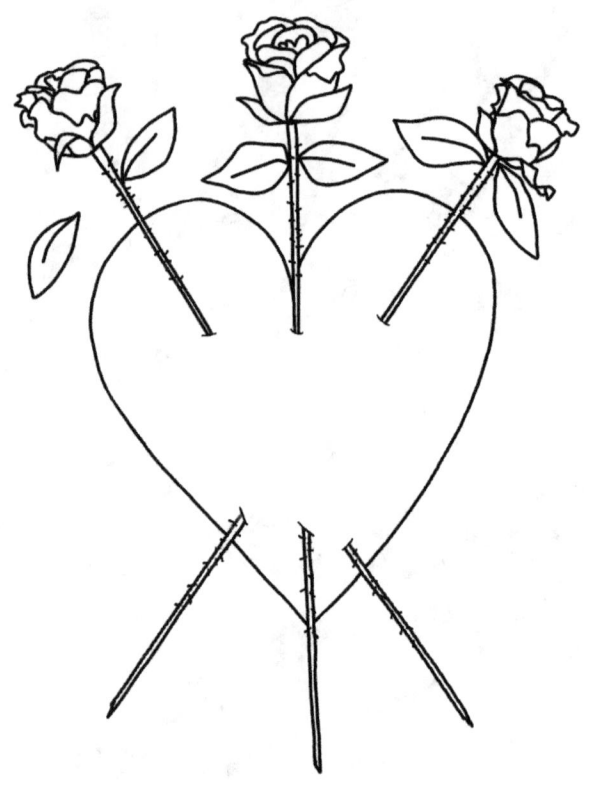

I am not here to solve the biggest problems in life
Or, teach anyone anything

I am here to embody love in its highest form
I am here to shine my light in its fullest luminosity
I am here to show and point at the beauty in this life and existence
I am a poet, lover, priestess
I am a warrior of the heart
Man and woman in one
Unity embodied
I am here to ride the waves and storms of emotion
To continuously survive every heartbreak
With even more capacity to love in my heart
I am not a God but his child
I am not a God but her child

I am one with the all and the all is me.

I AM HERE TO EMBODY LOVE.

There will never be as many days
As I'd like to tell you that I love you

There will never be the right words
The right amount of hugs
Kisses
Stares
For you to know
How loved you really are

And, I regret each day I am frozen by this fact and say nothing
Because my only wish is to pour out every ounce of love I feel for
you...

It scares me
How much one can feel
And somehow, maybe, the person you desperately want to feel what
you do, never will

And this is heartbreak

I hope my mother knows
How much I am going to miss her one day
Even though she is still here

I hope my father knows
That he is a beautiful man
With a heart of gold

I hope my brother knows
That I'm so proud of him
Every day

And I hope my lover knows
All the same, to this day

And last but not least, to myself
My first love

Perhaps the one that I neglect the most
I hope she knows how far I'd go
Just to let her know
That she is loved

No matter how far she may go
And no matter how many times she needs to grow

She is loved all the same
As all of the unspoken words

That she has yet to say...

Dearest Seeker,

The way is long, ever-unfolding, never ending. There is something at the end, the perceived one, the place we're all going. The way must not be approached by expecting shortcuts, loopholes, or, better yet, total bypassing of the way itself. There are no shortcuts, only death. What we are all seeking is not anything of this earth. It is the infinite light that embraces us upon passing. Reunification of the soul and the One. The truth is not found. It is.

The truth is not tangible, found in ancient tomes or tombs. It is the eternal now. The force inside all life. The intelligence of the cosmos, The love found between eye contact. The mysterious unraveling of everything. It is here. There is no seeking. Only being here now. In love.

Your permanent place of residence lies within. Is is always peaceful, safe, fun, clean, bright, loving, supportive, unshakable, calm, with laughter and abundance. You live here, and nothing can ever change that. When everything feels out of control, scary, unsafe, or negative, we can return home to this place inside. And then you recognize and remember this feeling, and take it with you.

It doesn't matter what or who shows up at your door. Thank them for coming by. And, depending on who's there, you choose to talk to, let in, or say no. Choose to share the love you feel within with everything you come into contract with. Because you know where you live, too. You have traveled to many places -- there is no doubt the terror and darkness that forever lurks. You learn from your experiences and question yourself over and over again. Until, you've seen enough. Then, it's time to come home.